MY FIRE'S GONE OUT!

How to cope with change in your work and your life.

Published by Accent Press Ltd – 2010

ISBN 9781907016516

With thanks to...

Sue, Dexter, J Girl, Roy, Trish, David Blount, Jen and remember Bryn you have ruined my life, only joking! Liam

To Jude and all the family. Thanks for sticking by me when times got tough. Martyn

To my mum Ann, and dad Ric, my girlfriend Tilly and my best mate Sy Wilderspin. We've all been through changes, many of which we've shared together and all of which have made our love for each other stronger. Peter

To my wife Diane, my three boys Elliott, Adam and Ethan, my mum, dad and brother Mark, Tony, Carol and Debbie, a big thanks for all your help and support over the years. Also thanks to all my friends who have been there for me and my family throughout the changes in my life. Thank you all. Steve

My Fire's Gone Out!

Foreword

Since I have written this book a number of major changes have happened to me in my life. Millions of people around the world have also experienced significant changes, some of them good some bad.

Change happens, it really does you know, but it is how we react to change that is important...

Keep your fire burning!

All illustrations by Steve Lilley
for more information visit: www.stevelilleydesign.co.uk

Fire video by 7video
for more information visit: www.7video.co.uk

My Fire's Gone Out!

Chapter 1

A long time ago, in a strange and dark world far beneath the earth, there lived four little devils who stoked the fires of hell.

It was hard work but most of the time they enjoyed what they did, after all it was a job wasn't it? And these days beggars can't be choosers. The devils in many ways were just like you and me; they had their strange quirks, their strengths, their weaknesses, their hopes and their worries. This is the story of how they reacted when sudden dramatic change interrupted their normal flow of life.

Why don't I introduce them to you...?

Sparky
A creative soul, Sparky is always coming up with new ideas. He loves having fun and grasping the many opportunities that life brings. Sparky has a positive can do attitude, is fast thinking and a bit quirky. Some people might say he is a little sensitive and doesn't like criticism, but then who does?

Oxy

Oxy is keen to get things done; he is very good with his hands and is always the first to get stuck in when something needs to be finished. He usually sees the bright side of life and would rather take action and complete a task than sit around talking about it all day. Some people might say Oxy is rigid and lives by rules and regulations, but that might be a bit harsh.

Diesel

A really deep thinker, Diesel is sound and reliable. You can always depend on him in a crisis. He will listen to both sides of an argument and make his own judgement. Some people might say he can be negative, a glass half-empty sort of person. But is that really the case, or is it just the thoughtful look on his face?

Stubbo

Stubbo has seen it all before; he tends to think that everything always goes wrong for him and has a negative attitude to life in general. He doesn't like change and prefers things to carry on just the same as they always have been. Some people might say he is one of life's victims, read on and make up your own mind!

Join the four devils, as they get ready to have their own world well and truly rocked!

Thoughts from the flames!

Everybody is different.
Learn to recognise, respect
and appreciate the people
around you.

Chapter 2

It was a morning very similar to many other mornings for the four devils. They were awoken by their alarm, got out of bed, had a quick shower, got dressed, made some breakfast, waved goodbye to their families and went to work.

They slowly made their way along the same twisting path through the dark and dimly lit caverns. As usual, at a crossroads, they would all meet – Sparky, Oxy, Diesel,

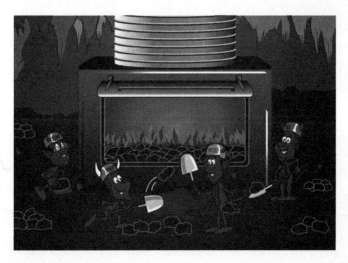

and Stubbo – and continue on their walk to work. Work began at the same time every day with the loud shrill of a siren. They started to shovel the fuel onto the furnace, to keep the fire burning.

They often had a laugh to make the time go quickly and after a lot of hard shovelling, a few coffee breaks and lunch in the rumour-mill canteen, before they knew it there was a long blast on the siren, and it was time to go home. They quickly made their way back along the path, through the caves to their families.

You see, not much changed in the world of the little devils, and it seemed to have a regular pattern and routine all of it's own.

Wake up, get ready, walk to work, start work, work hard, go home…

You can almost feel the rhythm as you repeat the words

Wake up, get ready, walk to work, start work, work hard, go home…

It was a similar routine every day and the devils were very comfortable and safe in the knowledge that they had work to pay their bills, look after their families and do the things that they enjoyed at night and at the weekends.

I suppose when you think about it, most of us are the same – we go to work, do our job and then go home – day in, day out, year in, year out, earning enough to do what ever makes us happy in our lives.

Generally we are all creatures of habit. We like things the way they are and don't like change. You might say we exist in our very own comfort zone and don't step outside of it very often. That's great isn't it as long as you're happy?

But change can sometimes happen when we least expect it!

Thoughts from the flames!

We all live by familiar routines
of one kind or another;
enjoy the moment and the
comfort they bring.

Chapter 3

It was a morning very similar to many other mornings for the four devils. Wait a minute... haven't you heard this somewhere before?

They were awoken by their alarms, got out of bed, had a quick shower, got dressed, made some breakfast, waved goodbye to their families and went to work.

They slowly made their way along the same twisting path through the dark caverns and caves. As usual, at the crossroads, they all met and continued on their familiar walk to work.

But this was going to be a different day!

When they arrived at work they saw a strange notice pinned to the wall. It read:

"By instruction of the management, the rumour-mill canteen is now closed. All devils are requested to use the new vending machine instead.

Biscuits will no longer be provided at meetings, and requests for new shovels should only be submitted in emergencies."

Now this caused quite a stir amongst the devils. Stubbo was all for laying down tools and walking out. Diesel wondered what the true meaning behind the words was. Oxy just wanted to start work and get on with it and Sparky was excited about what type of new drinks the vending machine would provide.

If I'm honest, these were just a few of the things the devils talked about. They went on about it for quite a long time until they began to get back to shovelling fuel and stoking the flames of the furnace.

It didn't take long until the notice was forgotten and after a few days they returned to their normal routine. Yes, there was the occasional chatter about the notice but it very quickly became business as usual.

Until a few weeks later, when Sparky mentioned that he had heard a rumour from another devil that their furnace might be in trouble and there was a chance they might be running out of fuel.

The other devils talked about this for a while until Stubbo said that at the end of the day it made no difference to them as they had loads of fuel and there was nothing to worry about. Sparky wasn't so sure though, he thought he had noticed their own fuel was running a bit low, he mentioned that as well but nobody really wanted to listen.

Thoughts from the flames!

Keep your eyes wide open as change is sometimes just around the corner.

My Fire's Gone Out!

Chapter 4

It was a morning very similar to many other mornings for the four devils ... I'm going to stop there, I'm sure you've heard enough of this by now ...

But it is important because, do you know what ...? This is going to be a very, very different day for the little devils, a day that will change their lives forever.

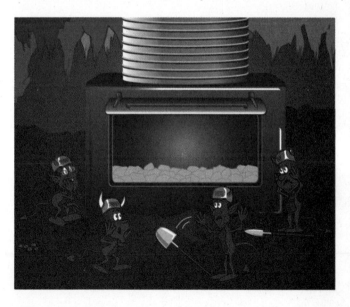

When they arrived at work the devils immediately noticed something was wrong. There was a strange musty, damp smell in the air and the cave seemed darker than usual.

In fact, it was so dark they couldn't even find the cupboard where they kept their shovels.

Then as the four devils walked to the furnace, they just stopped dead in their tracks and stared in absolute horror.

Their fire had gone out!

It is difficult to fully explain their reactions here, but I will try… from utter disbelief to despair, from hurt to anger. Their fire had gone out, their reason to come to work, the most important thing in their lives was gone, finished. The fire that fuelled their hopes, their families and their passion for life was extinguished.

All that was left was a few smouldering embers and even worse, Diesel had just noticed there was no longer any fuel left and there seemed no way they could re-light the fire!

They just stood there for what seemed like an eternity, gazing at the embers and thinking about what it would mean to them, their lives and their families.
No fire, no work – no fire, no fun.

What would the future bring?

Eventually they turned away from the embers and decided that there was nothing else to do but go home, except Stubbo, who was still staring in disbelief.

Thoughts from the flames!

Understand that change is constant, change happens!

Chapter 5

Let's stop and think for a minute here. If we are honest, whether at work or in our personal lives, sudden dramatic change is never easy to handle. But in the end we have to face up to the reality that change brings.

It was no different for the four devils, and at first they moped around at home, worrying and thinking, fretting and talking about what the fire going out meant to them. It affected them in many different ways and they certainly reacted in very different ways indeed.

Diesel took things very badly. He spent many hours worrying about what the future would bring. I need to let you into a secret here, Diesel had not been happy for quite a long time. Over the years he had built up a large amount of personal debt and each time a letter landed on his doorstep he worried that it might be yet another demand for payment. His concerns over his money problems were also having a negative affect on his family and friends. He was always snapping at somebody and seemed to be constantly miserable.

In fact, his soul was sinking long before the fire in the furnace had gone out. When he began to think about it, his own personal fire had gone out a long time ago, the flames being smothered by the heavy blanket of debt.

One day, as he was gazing through the window, he heard a knock on the door – it was Sparky and they had a long chat that seemed to go on for hours. Diesel told him about his worries and problems. Sparky was a good listener, he didn't give Diesel much advice, he just listened and listened and listened some more.

By the end of their chat Diesel felt strangely lighter, it was if he had lifted some of his worries just by talking to his old friend. He knew he had to do something and had wanted to for ages but he was frightened.

But now he knew he had to take action. He resolved to talk to the right people for advice and make a plan to repay the debts. He would even sell some of his most precious possessions if it meant he would be free of debt and worry. He talked it through with his family and within a few days he had agreed on a way forward.

He knew it wasn't going to be easy but he was determined he would succeed. He still didn't have a job, but the strange thing was that the flame going out in the furnace had forced him to address the other problems in his life.

Thoughts from the flames!

Change can be frightening –
talk about it with people who
are close to you and take
positive action to change
things for the better.

Chapter 6

The sudden change had hit all the devils hard, and it was no different for Stubbo. He was in a bad way, a very dark place indeed; I think I need to explain...

In the days immediately following the fire going out, Stubbo hadn't told his family what had happened and now every morning he continued with his same old routine. I think you know it by now...

Wake up, get ready, walk to work, start work, work hard, go home – it was the same as before except there was one major problem, there was no work!

No fire, no work - no fire, no fun.

Stubbo wanted to think that nothing had changed in his world; he wanted to believe that if he continued to do what he always did, then as if from nowhere, the fire would come back to life.

But the truth is, "If you do what you've always done, you'll get what you've always got."

And so, every day Stubbo just sat staring and staring at the cold, damp embers of the fire, hoping and wishing that everything would return to the way it had always been before. But it wasn't going to happen was it?

Let's take time to think about this for a moment... it is very easy to judge people and criticise people for their actions, but if we are honest, when a sudden dramatic change happens in life, it is not easy to predict how we will cope with it. Stubbo was in a state of shock. Everything that he knew, trusted and felt safe with had changed, he just didn't want to admit it.

But this is one of the most important messages from the tale of the four devils. It is not that change happens – we know it does, all the time – it is how we react to change; it is how we come to terms with the changes in our lives and do something about it, that makes a positive difference.

Unfortunately, Stubbo just kept on staring into the cold, damp embers of the fire and finally, slowly, sadly made his way home.

Thoughts from the flames!

Change happens constantly,
it is how we react to
change that is important.

My Fire's Gone Out!

38

Chapter 7

You will have probably realised by now that Sparky was generally a glass half-full sort of devil and in the weeks since the fire had gone out he had done lots and lots of thinking. He had taken the opportunity that the sudden change at work had given him, to reflect on his life and his future.

He had always been happy in his work but recently he was feeling as if something was missing; he couldn't quite understand exactly what it was, but something definitely wasn't right.

And strangely enough, he was feeling like that at home as well. Where he was usually full of energy and ideas, he had started to slip into a predictable routine. Everything was the same and nothing seemed new or interesting. Sparky was losing all his enthusiasm and drive; his personal fire wasn't burning very brightly at all.

He had been wondering for a while what was up with him – was it his age, his relationship with his partner, or just a phase that would pass by? Then, as suddenly as the fire went out at work, his personal fire started to slowly come back to life. Losing his job had forced him to think very deeply.

He asked himself three questions:

What was important to him in life?

What made him happy?

What was he passionate about?

He thought about the questions for quite a long time until he was happy with his answers. What was important to him was his family. At the end of the day, you could have the greatest job and all the money in the world, but if you don't have the love of people who are closest to you, you have nothing.

His family made him happy of course, but so did his friends, his hobbies – reading, music – and even his work, most of the time.

He was passionate about life in general really, if the truth be told. Doing new things, discovering new experiences, and living every day to the full. Just living really, just living...

Sparky soon realised that, for whatever reason, he had begun to close his eyes to the things that were really important to him in his life. When he finally opened them again he understood that they had been right there, staring at him all the time.

Ok, let's take time out here for a second or two...

In our own lives, would it be fair to say that we all go through times where we are down, unhappy and confused? That is normal; life is made up of highs and lows, the good and the bad. But when we are feeling low, do we ever ask ourselves the really important questions.

What is important to us in our lives?

What makes us happy?

What are we passionate about?

In truth, everybody will come up with his or her own individual answers. Some people will be able to answer them immediately and others might take hours or even days. Some answers will be similar, but the vital thing is that we ask the questions and focus on the things that are really important to us. In this crazy world we live in we often don't take time out to think about the really important things.

When you have thought about your own answers why not write them here.

What is important to you in your life?

What makes you happy?

What are you passionate about?

Sparky had already done a lot of thinking and understood now what was important to him, but the time for thinking was over. It was now time to go and grasp the opportunity that change had given him.

Thoughts from the flames!

Change can bring
opportunity –
ask yourself the
important questions.

Chapter 8

Sparky couldn't wait to tell his good friend Oxy what he had been thinking about and went straight over to see him.

Oxy was working hard in his garden when Sparky arrived. He always liked to keep himself busy, and even though the fire going out at work had really hit him hard, he knew that he had to keep himself occupied because at least it stopped him from worrying all the time.

But to be honest, he had been worrying – he had no job and no money, the fire had been his life and now it was gone. He knew he needed to do something for himself and his family but he just didn't know what that something was.

You see Oxy was a down-to-earth, hard working devil. He always did his best at the furnace and he knew that people could depend on him. He didn't often tell people, in case they thought he was a bit mad, but he loved his job and the sense of certainty and security that it gave him.

When the fire had gone out at work it had also started to go out in his personal life as well. He was happiest when he was busy doing something, but the problem was that the things to do at home were quickly running out.

When Sparky had told him everything he had been thinking about and explained all about the three important questions he had asked himself, a strange smile came across Oxy's face.

As soon as Sparky mentioned that change can be good and change can bring opportunity, it was almost as if he had been awoken from a deep sleep. It suddenly clicked; he knew what made him happy and what was really important to him in life. Yes, it was his family, but it was also his job at the furnace. Oxy loved the fun he had with his friends, the jokes and the pleasure of coming home after an honest day's work.

Their fire had gone out – yes – but there was no use just moaning about it, they had to do something to change things for the better.

They had to start looking for new fuel for the fire.

Oxy knew that this wasn't going to be easy as the caves and caverns went on for miles and miles and were dark and dangerous. Nobody had ever found any new fuel in the past but at least they could try couldn't they? At least they could give it a go.

The two devils began to enthusiastically plan for the future and were determined to start looking for the new fire first thing in the morning.

As Oxy went to sleep that night he felt a sense of calmness come over him. Their fire had gone out but they were going to do something about it.

Thoughts from the flames!

Take positive action
to change things
for the better.

My Fire's Gone Out!

Chapter 9

Oxy and Sparky didn't need their alarms the next morning; they literally jumped out of bed. They couldn't wait to get started and begin their search for the new fire.

They met up at the old crossroads where all the devils used to get together every morning before work, but instead of taking the normal turn in the road, they took a new direction and made their way down a different path.

They seemed to be walking for hours and hours down the dimly lit tunnels, every so often turning into a dark cave or a narrow opening. But no matter where they looked there was no sign of any fuel. This didn't stop them though, after all, they had only just started looking and there was plenty of time left in the day.

But the time soon ran out and they decided to return home and begin the search again in the morning. They searched and they searched for days and days but no matter how hard they looked they couldn't find the new fire.

Just like when they were at work, the quest for the fuel developed a routine all of its own.

Wake up, get ready, search for the fuel, go home.

Wake up, get ready, search for the fuel, go home.

The days soon turned into weeks and still they couldn't find the fuel for the fire. They were beginning to lose faith and all hope that they would ever find anything at all.

The doubts in their minds became bigger and more real with every passing day. What if there really wasn't any new fuel? What would they do? What would it mean to them and their families?

This was what was worrying Sparky as he was walking home with Oxy at the end of another disappointing day. He suddenly remembered some wise words that his mom had told him many years before, when he was a very young devil. She used to say to him:

"Sparky – you can, not you can't.

You will, not you won't.

If you have a dream, make the dream come true.

And never, ever give up…"

His mom was long gone now, but those inspiring words had shaped his whole life.

He began to scratch the words into the rock face. As Oxy started to read them out loud they echoed around the caves, finishing with the words:

"Never ever give up…

Never ever give up…

Never ever give up…"

He was absolutely determined now that they would find the fuel for the fire. He believed they would find it and he would do everything possible to make it happen. It was up to them, but perhaps they needed some help...it was time to go and talk to Diesel..

My Fire's Gone Out!

Thoughts from the flames!

If you believe, you will achieve, without belief you have nothing. If you have a dream make the dream come true!

Chapter 10

In the weeks that had passed since Diesel had told Sparky about his problems, things had seemed much better. He was a lot happier with himself and his family.

He was sticking to his plan to repay his debts and had sold some of his things to help begin to pay them off. He was really pleased to see Sparky again that morning; because he still had no job, he still had no fire.

Sparky explained that they had been searching for the new fuel for weeks, but no matter how hard they looked they couldn't find it any anywhere. It wasn't long before Diesel had agreed to help them and they soon set out again on their quest.

They again took a different direction into the caves and began walking and walking through the narrow passageways. The hours passed by and the devils were becoming tired and still they couldn't find a thing.

After searching for what seemed like an eternity they

were about to go home when suddenly, without saying a word, Diesel stopped and pointed to a strange, thin, green line in the rock.

After a moment he asked them if they had ever seen anything like it before. Oxy said he had seen something like it the other day but he hadn't given it much thought at the time because it was so small.

But this was different. It was a long, green line that got thicker and thicker as they moved deeper into the cave. The further they went, the bigger the green line became, until it started to glow brightly and began to cover the entire rock face. They followed it around the corner until they stopped in sheer amazement!

They couldn't believe their eyes. As far as they could see there was a mass of endless, green rocks dazzling and shining, almost blinding them with its brilliance.

Sparky held his breath, took out a match from his pocket, and picked up a piece of the green rock. He lit the match and held it against the rock… nothing happened. But then incredibly, the rock began to burn; slowly at first, then more brightly and then it became so hot and fierce that he had to put it down!

The devils shouted and danced with delight! They had found more fuel than they ever could have imagined. Better fuel, cleaner fuel and longer lasting fuel.

After all the time and effort they had spent looking, they had finally done it.

They could once again light their fire!

Thoughts from the flames!

Positive change can be just around the corner – never ever give up looking for it.

My Fire's Gone Out!

Chapter 11

Well, my tale of the little devils is nearly over – very nearly, but not quite. Let me just tie up a few loose ends for you.

The devils finally returned to work and once again began to stoke their new fire. They quickly got into their old routine; do you remember it?

Wake up, get ready, walk to work, start work, work hard, go home...

But things were very different this time. It was a new furnace, with better and longer lasting fuel, and most importantly, each of the devils felt and thought differently.

I suppose you could say that the devils had become stuck in a rut and were complacent with their old routine. They didn't recognise this until the fire went out at work and forced them to examine their own lives. They had learnt a lot, not only about how to cope with change at work, but also about their personal lives.

Sparky was in love with life again and had got his old enthusiasm back. Diesel had come to terms with his personal problems and was now working his way through his plan to clear his debt. And Oxy – well, Oxy was just Oxy – happy to be back at work with his friends and earning money to support his family. But you know what...? You never heard him complain about work ever again.

There was one other very important thing though. The devils were determined never to let their fire go out ever

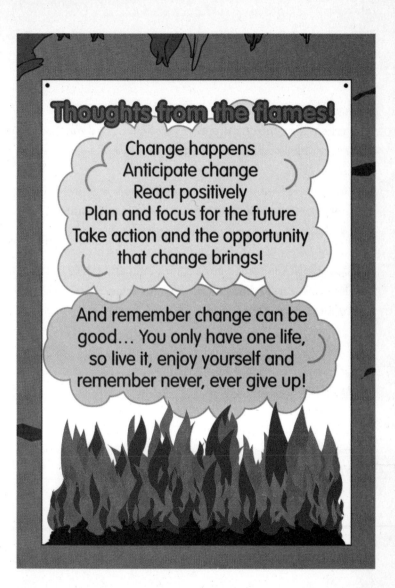

again. They always kept their eyes wide open, checking to see that there was still plenty of fuel left.

To help them remember the lessons they had learned from the fire, they put up a special 'Thoughts from the flames!' poster on the rock face…

I would like to say that the story ends on a high here as most good tales do, but I am afraid it doesn't quite finish like that. What had happened to Stubbo?

Well, all the devils had gone to find him and tell him about the new fuel for the fire and the amazing caves and furnace they had found, but he just wasn't interested and turned away.

Rumour has it that Stubbo still goes to the old furnace day after day, month after month, and just sits sadly staring and staring in to the cold, dark embers of the furnace. Waiting and waiting for the fire

to spark back into life and things to change back to the
way they used to be.

Sitting and staring.

Waiting and waiting.

And waiting and waiting and waiting...

Chapter 12

The story behind the fire!

After we had finished writing 'My fire's gone out', we felt it might be useful to give you some background on how we came up with the idea for the book in the first place; what it meant to us both personally and in business. Here goes then:

I was on my way to do a keynote presentation in London, with Peter and Martyn, who were going to be filming at the same event. I was a little bit down at the time… strange you might think, for a motivational speaker. There were quite a few changes that I was making with my business, and if I'm truthful, I think I had probably lost my focus on what was really important. After all, who motivates the motivator? You I suppose, but anyway back to the story…

As we drove along and chatted, we talked about various different ideas. We began to talk about working together on a book about change. In the late nineties I had been inspired by the book 'Who moved my cheese' by Dr Spencer Johnson, and for many years I had wanted to write my own story about change. I wanted to create the new 'cheese' if you like.

By this time we had already set up a new business called Little Devils, and as we continued to talk through the idea, Martyn suddenly said, "Why don't we call it 'My fire's gone out' and not only talk about dealing with business change but talk about personal change as well? How you react when your personal flame is burning a little low and you are down and confused."

The metaphor "My fire's gone out" had obviously sparked Martyn, literally sparked him as it happened. He had linked devils to fire and fire to 'My fire's gone out', and then finally, to business and personal change.

We were totally inspired and that night we immediately sat down and started to sketch out the characters. Sparky, Stubbo, Diesel and Oxy were quickly born, along with an outline plan for the book.

Over the next few months we continued to meet and work on the story until finally it was finished.

Pictured: Liam O'Connell, Martyn Harris, Steve Lilley and Peter Sims.

The amazing thing was that as we were writing, it had an incredibly positive affect on us all.

I began to re-examine my focus and made a number of big changes to my business. I had gone down a particular route and it wasn't working as well I would have liked, so I decided to change again and go back to what I loved and was successful at; inspiring people to create great businesses and lives and cope with the ever-changing world we live in.

As soon as I regained my focus and decided to change things, my business flourished and even better, I was happier. My wife Sue was happier, even my golden retriever Dexter was happier! I just needed the catalyst for change and to open my eyes and focus on what I was good at in the first place.

As the book was coming to life, Martyn, Peter and Steve also reflected on their own businesses and lives.

Martyn had worked in media for many years; he enjoyed his work but sometimes felt frustrated with the everyday rules and regulations. One rainy August afternoon he was out on a job with me and was having a moan that things were not going well at work. His fire had gone out.

After listening to Martyn I said, "Why don't you do something about it? It's up to you, it's your life."

Within six months Martyn had started up his own business with Peter. He had left a secure job but as he says, "At the end of the day it is not just about the money – yes, that is important – but it's how you feel when you get up every morning."

"If you aren't happy, change things… look for something new… be happy. After all you only have one life!"

Peter was having a really bad time; you could say his fire had well and truly gone out. He said it was so bad that he still seemed to be "pouring water on it" himself. In the space of a few months he had split up with his girlfriend, fallen out with his parents and a close member of his family had been diagnosed with cancer.

For a time he was totally down, but he found that working on the concepts for 'My fire's gone out' really helped him to plan for the future and focus on the opportunities that life and work bring.

If he was honest, the one thing he hadn't done was anticipate change, but we are only human and we continue to learn as we go along. The changes in his life helped him look again at what was really important. The great news is his relationship with his parents is now stronger than it has ever been.

Peter says, "Every day tell the people close to you that you love them; enjoy the moment because you can't always predict the future."

Steve had been working in the advertising industry for many years as a graphic designer. After being made redundant once before, he quickly found a new job with another design and PR agency. After working there happily for several years, the agency unfortunately lost a major client and Steve soon noticed the drop in workload.

In much the same way as the devils had seen the warning signs of change coming, Steve could see his fire was soon to go out! So he decided to do something about it and started up his own design company.

When the inevitable did happen and he was made redundant from the agency, he had everything in place ready to work full-time for himself. As the thoughts from the flames say, "It is important to keep your eyes wide open, as change can be just around the corner."

Although it was challenging building up the business, he knew that the end rewards would be worth it, and five years down the line his business is still going strong.

Steve says, "In life we all come to a crossroads for change in one way or another, be it in our career or in our personal lives. Following a new path of change can be a little scary at first but for me it was for the better. Now I can spend more time with my family and I am more motivated at work."

We passionately hope that this book helps people to cope with change, whatever it might be, in business or life. There are many different relevant areas that it touches:

Business change – mergers, restructuring, reorganisation.

Personal change – new job, new relationships, life's many challenges.

In fact it applies to any change really, and we have adapted the 'thoughts from the flames' in the book to reflect not only our experience in business, but also the universal themes of common sense and the reality of life in general.

And as I write this final paragraph, we are suffering probably the deepest recession that the world has seen for many years. It is a difficult time but times change, and in the end, it is how we deal with adversity that really matters.

Remember… **keep your fire burning!**